I Walked to the Bus Stop

Copyright © 2020 Kay Reynolds
All rights reserved
First Edition

PAGE PUBLISHING, INC.
Conneaut Lake, PA

First originally published by Page Publishing 2020

ISBN 978-1-64628-777-2 (pbk)
ISBN 978-1-64628-778-9 (digital)

Printed in the United States of America

I Walked to the Bus Stop

KAY REYNOLDS

I walked to the bus stop,
Happy for the day.
Going to see my grandma
And spend the night away.
I looked up to the sky
To see the beautiful sun,
It was then that I realized,
There was but one.

The bus finally arrived,
I got on and said, "Hi."
I looked around to find a seat,
Anywhere close by.
No one was on board, so any seat would do.
It was then that I realized,
There was now two.

A lady got on the bus

At the very next stop.

She wore a huge hat

That matched her yellow top.

She dropped her coins to pay her fee,

It was then that I realized,

There was now three.

The bus stopped again,
And one more got on.
This time, a man
Who was on his phone.
He ended his call and sat by the door.
It was then that I realized,
There was now four.

My stop was next,
And I would walk awhile.
But when the doors opened,
I was greeted with a smile.
It was Grandma and Grandpa
With two cousins by their side.
It was then that I realized,
There was now five.

Hugs all around

And lots of love to share.

Hand in hand, we walked along,

Jumping around with no care.

A stray dog came up to give us some licks,

It was then that I realized,

There was now six.

We walked for a while,
And the puppy followed us home.
We skipped, jumped, laughed, and played
While the puppy carried his bone.
As we entered into Grandma's gate,
I petted her cat named, Kevin.
It was then that I realized,
There was now seven.

Walking through the yard,

Admiring her roses so red,

The cutest little bluebird

Pounced upon my head.

Startled and excited, I stood up tall and straight,

It was then that I realized,

There was now eight.

An exciting day was shared,
And the sun was setting low,
Only an hour left of fun
Before bath time we would go.
I decided to take a walk
To feed Grandpa's only swine,
It was then that I realized,
There was now nine.

With the whole group together,

I started counting each one off.

I patted each head

As I choked back a cough.

Going 'round the circle, including Grandma's red hen,

It was then that I realized,

There was now ten.

What a super day I had, and I was very tired,
We ate together and shared our day,
Which lasted for a while.
Off to bathe and into bed to sleep the night away,
As I drifted into dreamland about the day of fun,
It was then that I realized,
There was but one.

Good night!

About the Author

As a mother of three and Gigi (grandmother) of eight, Kay Reynolds has a heart for children and knows the importance of wholesomeness in literature. For many years, Kay has worked around books by being a current full-time employee at Florida Schoolbook Depository in Jacksonville, Florida, that houses and ships books to schools and different venues throughout the state. Kay would love nothing more than to direct children into a love of listening and reading stories to boost their intellect and allow them to "dream big." What started as a mere hobby of putting words on paper has blossomed into so much more, and if becoming an author can happen to her, it can also be a reality for you as well. She would love to connect with her readers, so please feel free to reach out to her at kaybelle45@gmail.com to give her feedback and let her know your thoughts for future stories. God bless you and may He touch and inspire you through the written Word.